PROPHETIC ZONE OF WAR

PROPHETIC ZONE OF WAR

BY

KERVIN DIEUDONNE

iUniverse, Inc.
Bloomington

PROPHETIC ZONE OF WAR

iUniverse books may be ordered through booksellers or by contacting:

iUniverse
1663 Liberty Drive
Bloomington, IN 47403
www.iuniverse.com
1-800-Authors (1-800-288-4677)

ISBN: 978-1-4759-7524-6 (sc)
ISBN: 978-1-4759-7525-3 (ebk)

Printed in the United States of America

iUniverse rev. date: 02/05/2013

TABLE OF CONTENT

INTRODUCTION

All the Bible verses from this book were taking from the
NKJV Bible unless noted otherwise.

At the age of 8, I witnessed my father perform
deliverances, through the casting out of demons and
breaking satanic curses upon various people; he did
all of this in the name of Jesus Christ. I recall how I became very
fearful of the devil from witnessing people being delivered
from demonic forces. Because of my limited knowledge of
the Word of God, fear consumed my life; as a result I was
in bondage for almost 20 years. Hosea 4:6 states "My people
are destroyed, for lack of knowledge" (KJV). Satan is able
to put you into bondage due to your lack of knowledge of
God's word; which is how he was able to keep me bound. If I
had knowledge of the word of God, I would not have been in
bondage for so long.

Fear of the Devil causes unbelief in the power of God. In
order for you to be set free from bondage, you must identify
and apprehend what areas of your life you are in bondage
and who has done it. Satan tries to bring fear into your life and
demonstrate that he has power over you. Fortunately, once
you gain an understanding of who Satan is and the power he
claims to have, you will overcome your fear of him.

In this book, by the grace of God and through the revelation
of the Holy Spirit, God will reveal to you Satan's identity. You
cannot fight what you cannot see; you must know how to
fight your enemy. First we are going to study the history of
Satan and why he was cast out of heaven. Then we will study
the different elements we battle against found in the book

of Ephesians. Lastly, we will encounter the different battle styles or techniques to engage into battle according to your situation.

As you read this book I pray in the name of Jesus Christ that deliverance will begin to enter your house, your life and your family; that the fire of God will come upon you. In addition, I pray that God will begin to move in your life in a fresh way, and that you begin to come out of bondage by fire in the name of Jesus. In John 8:32 Jesus says "And ye shall know the truth and the truth shall set you free" (KJV). There is liberty to those who come to know Christ, who is the truth. The Holy Spirit is about to expose the devil to you; the enemy that has been in your backyard keeping you in bondage.

By the end of this book I DECREE AND DECLARE IT BY THE PROPHETIC AUTHORITY that you are set free in every area of your life where Satan has kept you in bondage or captivity, in Jesus name. As you finish reading this book, in the Name of Jesus, let the anointing that destroy yokes, voodoo, witchcraft, magic, hexes, vexes, jinxes, incantations, enchantments, hoodoo, or any power of the enemy, let that anointing manifest as you read and begin to flow in you and set you free in the mighty name of Jesus. For whom the Son has set free, is free indeed (John 8:36 *KJV*)

Prayer

Father God, I plead the Blood of Jesus Christ over myself, my home, family and possessions. I cover myself under the Blood of Jesus from every spirit that would intend to attack me because of this book; I break the power of any confusion the enemy has sent against me. I take authority over every demon of the sea, earth, air and water that would try to come against me. I bind them and send them into the abyss in the mighty name of Jesus. May the fire of God fall upon me and may I receive the mind of Christ in Jesus mighty name, Amen.

Part One

---·◈·---

The fall of Satan

How you are fallen from heaven, O Lucifer, son of the morning! How you are cut down to the ground, you who weakened the nations!

Isaiah 14:12 (NKJV)

1

ANGELS

Are they not all ministering spirits sent forth to
minister for those who will inherit salvation?

Hebrews 1:14 NKJV

Before we begin I would first like to introduce to you the different types of angels and their functions. There are three types of powerful angels revealed throughout scriptures; the Worship, Messenger, and Warrior Angels. The leaders of these angels are Archangels Michael, Gabriel and formally Lucifer; each of them had a third of the angels assigned to them. Archangel Michael leads the warrior angels (Revelation 12:7), Archangel Gabriel leads the messenger angels (Luke 1:19-20), Lucifer at that time, led the worship angels (Revelation 12:4) (Ezekiel 28:13).

Worship angels; the Cherubim and Seraphim are angels that reverence and adore God. In the bible we find them in God's presence worshipping him every day. In the book of revelation the bible says the elders fell to worship God there were four living creatures that worshipped him as well accompanied by a host of angels that did the same.

Messenger angels bring the Word of the Lord to us. We find in the bible in the book of Daniel in chapter 8 where a messenger Angel spoke to Daniel. Daniel prayed and fasted for 21 days waiting on a messenger angel to bring to him the revelation or the message of the vision that he had receive from the Lord. According to scriptures an angel of Satan fought with the messenger angel attempting to stop him from delivering the message to Daniel. Archangel Michael had to contend on behalf of the messenger angel so the message could be delivered to Daniel.

Warrior angels fight our battles. According to scriptures in the story of Joshua, upon Joshua's arrival to Jericho a warrior angel appeared to him to fight alongside him. Warrior angels are the ones who engage in spiritual warfare on our behalf, they are always ready to fight for Jesus. Many times God releases our enemies into the hands of the warrior angels. All angels play a specific role in the spiritual realm, each one in their rightful and respectable places.

2

SATAN VS. MAN

*You were perfect in your ways from the day you were
created, till iniquity was found in you*

Ezekiel 28:15 (NKJV)

In the book of Ezekiel 28:12, the Bible describes the fall of Satan, and events prior to that regarding his position. According to the Bible, Lucifer (Satan) was a model of perfection, full of wisdom and perfect in beauty. The power that was in the hand of Satan was very great; God ordained Lucifer and anointed him to serve. He was blameless in the eyes of God, until wickedness was found in him (Ezekiel 28 *NKJV*). According to Ezekiel chapter 28, Lucifer became filled with inner violence and sinned; his jealousy towards God consumed him.

Satan was anointed and ordained to work on the earth; his responsibility was to protect the Garden of Eden and everything therein. God placed Satan as the Guardian of the Garden of Eden, giving him access and authority over the earth (Ezekiel 28). His ordination was not for heaven, but for the earth. During that time the Word of God had not yet become flesh, Satan was the one who had a ministry on earth. The anointing of The Holy Spirit is not for heaven, it is for earth. The purpose of the anointing is to destroy yokes (Isaiah 10:27) and anything that tries to attack the children of God. In heaven there are no yokes. In heaven we will be in the

5

Glory realm at all times, there is no need for the anointing in heaven. In order for Satan to have access on earth God had to anoint him and ordain him (Ezekiel 28:14) so he can serve in his ministry.

Lucifer knew the plan of God for mankind even before God created man. Lucifer was still serving in the presence of God he was not out of heaven yet when he discovered the plan for mankind. Lucifer was jealous that God planned to create a being in *His* (God) own image, one in *His* likeness. Lucifer, like all angels was not created in the image of God, but God planned to do this for mankind. Lucifer was envious of man. Man being created in the image of God meant they would contain the attributes of God. We (humankind) are the mirror of God himself; we resemble God while the angels do not.

Lucifer's jealousy fed his pride and he desired to be higher than God. His plan was to steal the power that God placed in man. He figured that if he could obtain the power of man, which is the power of God Himself (John Chapter 10), he could overthrow God. Lucifer said to himself that if he could tempt Man and get the power in man then he would ascend to heaven and raise his throne above the stars of God (Isaiah 14:13).

Upon God's creation of Man in the book of Genesis, Lucifer was still serving God and was not yet cast down. In his arrogance Lucifer devised a plan and deceived the third of the angels that were in his command. He led them to believe that he was going to overthrow God and that he would give them powers, kingdoms and places to control. He began to show them the moon, the sun, the heavens, the lightning, the thunders, the tornados, the hurricane, the floods, the sea, the waters, the rivers, the mountains, the desserts, the hills, the forests, the cold places, the earth, the underneath of the earth, the air and the fire kingdom which is located in the center of the earth. So they saw the goods, then he laid the plan before them and the angels followed him.

According to Revelation chapter 12, Archangel Michael stepped up and began to fight against Satan. The Bible states that the devil was not strong enough to fight back, so he was hurled unto the earth. Satan was cast out of heaven because he thought that he could steal God's power. He thought he could steal the fullness of the Spirit placed in Man and overthrow God. The Bible declares in Revelation Chapter 12, that Satan was hurled unto the earth and the children of the earth must be aware because he is furious. He is angry and will torment those that are on the earth.

3

THE PREDATOR

The thief does not come except to steal,
and to kill, and to destroy

John 10:10a

God gave us the warning concerning the enemy who is living among us. The three major natures of Satan are to steal, kill and destroy, but Jesus Christ came to give us life and life more abundantly. As the bible declares lack of Knowledge my people are perishing, The Lord has given us a warning concerning the enemy that is amongst us. The Lord warns us about him, He told us to be very careful concerning Satan for he seeks to deceive. The same technique that he used to deceive one third of the Angels that were in heaven and Adam and Eve, is the same technique he will use with us.

Satan even tried to deceive Jesus Christ with his lies, but the Lord was aware of Satan's schemes. Satan lives in our midst, he seeks to torment the people of God. We are surrounded by wickedness and evil, but if we allow the Holy Spirit to impregnate us with the Revelation of Jesus Christ then we will be able to destroy and overpower the plans of the Enemy. We will walk from one step of Glory to another step of Glory. You need to understand what you are fighting against, know your enemy, his tactics, his strategic movement, his smell, his voice, his touch, how he dresses, how he looks and his attitude.

You need to know everything about him. Before you can fight against your enemy you need to seek knowledge concerning him first. The way to obtain knowledge about your enemies is through revelation from the Holy Spirit. You will begin to ask the Holy Spirit to reveal it to you.

Demons live all around us; there is no where in this world you can go that there are no demons. Without Spiritual warfare there is no way you can win against them. Satan is afraid of believers who engage in spiritual warfare; believers who stand and fight against him in the name of Jesus. Satan does not like believers who apply Luke 10:19. To engage into warfare you need a better view and understanding of it, the Holy Spirit will expose the devil to you as you read this, and The Holy Spirit will teach you various ways of how to engage into spiritual warfare, and a better UNDERSTANDING OF SPIRITUAL WARFARE

Prayer

Father in the name of Jesus, set me free from captivity, bondage, deceptions, lies and the schism of the enemy in the name of Jesus. Father in the name of Jesus where ever my destiny, blessings, marriage, gifts, family, or anything that I have been praying for lies; whether it be in the moon, the sun, the heavens, the sea, the waters, the rivers, the mountains, the desserts, the hills, the forest, the cold places, the earth, underneath the earth, the air and the fire kingdom I command them to come out by fire in the name of Jesus, according to Luke 10:19. Right now come out of there in the name of Jesus, right now by fire in Jesus name. Today let the deliverance anointing come upon me and set me free from these camps and kingdoms of the enemy in the name of Jesus Christ. In the name of Jesus I am free and I receive it today by fire in Jesus name, Amen.

Part Two

Authority over the Elements

Behold, I give you the authority to trample on serpents and scorpions, and over all the power of the enemy, and nothing shall by any means hurt you.

Luke 10:19 (NKJV)

1

Spiritual Warfare

In The book of Ephesians, Apostle Paul addresses spiritual warfare (Ephesians 6:12) for our struggle is not against flesh and blood, but against the principalities, rulers, powers and spiritual forces of evil in the heavenly realms. We are not fighting against one another, but Apostle Paul explains we are fighting against the Spirits; the 4 spirits mentioned in Ephesians 6:12. Those Spirits are four powerful tools or weapons of the devil that we need to be aware of and understand.

To understand Spiritual warfare, we must understand the four spirits in the four Elements of this world. The devil took the earth from Adam and Eve and established his Kingdom over this earth by using the things of the earth to torment the people of God. We are going to take a deeper look at each one of them, and expose the devil through all four demonic spirits we find in Ephesians 6:12. Be ready, put on your armor, so we can enter into the Realm of Spiritual warfare, say "Enough Satan, no more devil for I am dressed in my suit of War". No worries Jesus never loses a fight. Now enter the realm of spiritual warfare in the mighty name of Jesus Christ.

2

FOUR DEMONIC STRONGMEN

Apostle Paul describes the four demonic spirits we fight against every day; the Prince of the Air, the Powers, the Rulers, and the wicked forces or spirits. Demonic spirits dominate the world we are living in. We must deal with them on a daily base to win the fight against spiritual warfare. All these spirits are connected to an element of this world, in a corporate effort to keep the people of God in Bondage.

There are four elements on earth; air, water, earth and fire. Without these elements we cannot live on this planet. We need all four elements to survive on earth, if one were missing it would be a problem for humanity. In order for Satan to have access in our lives he assigns spirits according to those elements to control them; by doing so he keeps the people of God in bondage on a daily base. The Air element is controlled by the Prince of the Air; the Water Element is controlled by the Powers; the Earth Element is controlled by the Rulers; and the fire Element is controlled by the wicked forces or spirits. Everybody has at least one if not all four of these spirits to deal with. Satan plans everything well, so he can keep the Children of God in Bondage, but we bless God for the Spirit of Revelation which is Jesus Christ.

3

PRINCIPALITY OR AIR SPIRITS

There are 3 heavens: the first one is the one we see every day, the second one is where Satan (Genesis 1:6 *KJV*), the Prince of the air and his angels dwell and the third heaven is where God the Father, God the Son and God the Holy Spirit dwell along with the elect and holy angels. In the second heaven, dark angels (unholy angels), rebellious and satanic angels remain there; when they come down, they come to destroy. Some voodoo priests serve these kinds of angels as their gods, for example the queen of heaven; some people believe she is the mother of Jesus. She is one of the dark angels that voodoo priests serve. They remain in the second heaven operating in ways to deceive people; one of the ways they deceive people are through familiar spirits.

Some Christians believe they are moving in the gift of God but it is a familiar spirit. Dark angels move in the Air, according to Hebrews chapter one God made his angels as wind and his servants as flames of fire. The dark angels are wind, at times they tap into our dreams to try and confuse us, deceiving us into believing its God speaking to us. Some people are bound in the second heaven and their destiny and blessings remain there because of the dark angels. If you are not into spiritual warfare you will not be able to stop them or be free from them you need to recognize them through discernment. With discernment you will know how to deal with them when they appear in your life. The bible tells us that Satan is an angel of light; he has the ability to disguise himself as a holy angel. Without discernment, you will not know how to free yourself from Satan. Satan will deceive you and fight against you, to kill your destiny.

Many times principalities or air spirits hold some of the things we pray for or they fight against our messenger angels. In the bible we see where Daniel fasted for 21 days to receive his blessing but the Prince of Persia (principality or air spirit) delayed the arrival of his blessing. In the second heaven there is a satanic system established, in this establishment principalities or air spirits war against our angels to delay or take our messages or blessings away. Many times we pray for God to do certain things in our lives and we never see it come to pass, that is a result of the air spirits holding our blessings, which is what happened to Daniel.

The dark angels in the second heaven dominate the moon and sun. In the first heaven they dominate rain, lightning, tornados, hurricanes, thunder etc. If you do not take authority over them, these spirits will use these forces against you. Some people, who practice witchcraft, utilize the moon, the sun, the first heaven, rain, lightning, hurricanes, thunder, tornados etc; if you do not take authority upon them the enemy will attack you through them; that is the power using the element of Air. We must have our eyes open concerning these dark angels and fight back by fire. Open your spiritual eyes to understand the things that are around you and enter into the realm of spiritual warfare to destroy the plans and works of the prince of the air. Those principalities are aware of you, but are you aware of them. We are going to pray to break that power and to take authority over the element of the air, where ever you go in Jesus' mighty name

Prayer

Father in the name of Jesus, I pray according to Luke 10:19 with the authority you have giving to me to destroy the work of the enemy, I destroy every weapon that has fashion against me, every tongue

spoke against me must be put to confusion in the mighty name of Jesus. I pray that every power from the air that is attacking my life, loose your hold in the name of Jesus fall down and be disgraced in Jesus Christ of Nazareth's Mighty name. Today I claim my victory from you in the name of Jesus Amen.

4

POWERS OR WATER SPIRITS

Then one of the seven angels who had the seven bowls
came and talked with me, saying to me¹ "Come, I will
show you the judgment of the great harlot who sits
on many waters, ² with whom the kings of the earth
committed fornication, and the inhabitants of the earth
were made drunk with the wine of her fornication."

Revelation 17:1-2

There are times where God will take me in the realm of the spirit and bring me under the sea. While I am there he shows me people whose spirits are bound under water by the sea people. In the book of Revelation chapter 17 it gives an account of a water spirit, it describes the woman who sat on the beast; she had a golden cup she drunk from, that was full of wickedness. Without the spirit of God, you can become a victim of the water spirit. Only Jesus Christ can deliver a person who is bound there. Water spirits hinder the growth of many ministries. A spirit of Prayer is needed, for you to contend against them.

Apostle Paul spoke of powers which are the spirits under the Sea; these spirits operate under the water. According to various studies, over 60% of the Human Body is made up of water; spiritually this gives water spirits access to attack us, if we do not take authority over them. The water spirits include but are not limited to: the Marine Kingdom, spirit of Wife or

Husband, incubus, succubus, Leviathan, Queen of the Coast or Queen of the rivers etc. Many people in this world fight against these spirits, but they do not know how to attack it.

Water spirits are known to destroy marriages, businesses and churches; they bring sickness, confusion, pride, lust, perversion, sexual immorality, adultery, fornication, sex addiction, heaviness and much more. Water spirits attack and destroy the lives of believers, and it is not a spirit that we should mess around with. Prayer, fasting and the word of God is needed to fight this.

Prayer

Father in the name of Jesus Christ, I humble myself before your throne, through the blood of Jesus. I repent of every sin that I have committed that gave access to water spirits to enter my life. By the blood of Jesus I renounce every covenant, every curse, and every contract with that spirit I renounce and break them over my life, my family, ministry, marriage, house, finances, children, businesses, and everything that belongs to me. Any area of my life this spirit has attacked I destroy it by fire in the name of Jesus Christ of Nazareth. any links, relationship, marriages, friendship with water spirits incubus, succubus, spirit of wife or husband, spiritual children, satanic woman, queen of the coast, woman from the waters, witches I break and destroy it in the name of Jesus Christ, by the blood of Jesus Christ I declare freedom in the name of Jesus Christ.

5

RULERS OR EARTH SPIRITS

*'Why did the nations rage and the people plot vain
things? The kings of the earth took their stand and the
rulers were gathered together against the LORD and
against His Christ.*

Acts 4:25-26 NKJV

Jesus said that we live in this world but we are not of this world (John 15:19), Jesus said here comes the prince of this world but he found nothing in me (John 14:30). The devil stole this world from us and established his kingdom. Many times when you do something in this world you have to go through the plots of the devil, steal, lies, hatred, fights, jealousy, etc. The devil does all of this so Christians can fall and not follow the word of God or his plan for their lives.

We cannot place our trust in the things of this world. The day you do so, the devil will receive access to your heart to attack you and slow you down from serving God. Some people place their trust in their job which can take them out of church; other people place their trust in a car; some people place it in a house, some people its money, husband, wife, a child or entertainment. We must be careful of what we do in this world and serve God with our whole heart, in spirit and in truth. We must not allow the Devil to deceive us with lies, wealth or things of this world. We need to follow the directions of God. We are more than a conqueror when we understand the system of this world and when we understand the enemy we are fighting with.

Many times disembodied spirits (spirits without bodies) work with earth spirits; they seek for a body to operate or possess. The devil has kingdoms over this earth, camp sites, secrets societies, governments, authorities, markets, stores, police, churches, pastors, workplaces, businesses, etc. Many Government officials, Kings and Presidents work for the devil. The Devil has placed a system over this world that most of us fall into. We cannot trust the system of this world nor fall for it. Jesus said the enemy seeks to steal, kill and destroy. We must fight and declare war against the system of this World and preach the good news of Jesus Christ. Jesus said go and preach the good news every where around the world. The devil has agents all over the world. Open your eyes people and look around you, fight the kingdom of darkness and destroy it through Jesus Christ.

Prayer

O lord why do kings of the earth plot against your anointed ones? By fire in the name of Jesus we put them to shame. we come against the system of this world and the plan we put confusion in the name of Jesus Christ of Nazareth every spirits in the businesses, stores, schools, jobs, houses, neighborhoods, governments, everywhere around this earth we rebuke them in the mighty name of Jesus Christ we destroy every arrows set up against us in the name of Jesus. Every king and prince against our lives in the mighty name of Jesus we have come against you, in the name of Jesus Christ, loose your hold. I speak divine favor in the name of Jesus Christ amen.

6

WICKED SPIRITS OR FIRE KINGDOM

At the name of Jesus every knee should bow, of those in
heaven, and of those on earth, and of those under the
earth, and that every tongue should confess that Jesus
Christ is Lord, to the glory of God the Father.

Philippians 2:10-11NKJV

W icked spirits are bound underneath the earth. They seek to destroy our lives. The spirits in the Fire Kingdom are not controlled by the devil. Some spirits are bound in the bottomless pit of the earth or the tuataras, or Gehenia. The Fire Kingdom contains those spirits; God chained and bound them in hell according to Revelation 13:11-18, the creature has the power to perform miracles, perform signs and wonders and call fire from heaven. We need to be careful, these wicked spirits will seek to destroy and deceive you claiming they are God. They claim they can give you powers and make you their prophets. They teach you false doctrines and have you worship their carved images.

In Haiti they are known as LOUA (Haitian Gods and Goddesses). Those spirits are attached in pictures, talismans, pictures in shirts, stuffed animals and dolls. Those spirits desire to be worshipped like God. They seek for servants and blood. They turn families against each other; causing siblings to kill each other. They have different tactics which include possessing human beings, and transforming into animals. They have their own symbol, shrines, priests and signs. We must be careful of the company we choose to be around sometimes they are servants of these spirits. We need to fight against those spirits and bind them in the mighty name of Jesus.

Prayer

In the name of Jesus, Father I thank you for your grace and the blood of Christ. In the name of Jesus I bind every wicked spirit, idol, image, talisman, satanic priest and satanic prophets fashioned against my life. I put them to confusion and destruction in the name of Jesus Christ of Nazareth. I destroy the power of the enemy and bind them to Tatarus in the mighty name of Jesus Christ of Nazareth, Amen.

7

DELIVERANCE FROM
THE ELEMENTS

*Put on the whole armor of God that you may be able to
stand against the wiles of the devil.*

Ephesians 6:11NKJV

We need to fight and declare war with those spirits that work in the elements and destroy their attacks against our lives. Everyone has some where one of these elements has placed their destiny or future. You need to fast and pray that God may reveal to you where the enemy is attacking your life and through which elements. At times we suffer because we do not know what we are doing. Hosea 4:6 (NKJV) says—*My people are destroyed for lack of knowledge,* we need the knowledge, the word of God. In order to be victorious we need to be aware of the enemy. It is time to wake up, and seek for where your destiny, blessing, future, marriage, and finance are hidden.

It is time to receive a revelation from the Holy Spirit, so you may know where in these four elements the devil has taken what God has given to you. It is when you war against these spirits and gain victory through Christ Jesus that you receive your deliverance; renouncing any covenant or agreement you may have had with them.

Part Three

---∞---

Weapons of Warfare

Finally, my brethren, be strong in the Lord and in the power of His might. [11] Put on the whole armor of God, that you may be able to stand against the wiles of the devil.

Ephesians 6:10-11 (NKJV)

INTRODUCTION

There are 3 different ways we can fight the enemy: challenging battle, processing battle and strategic battle. Many times people are unable to pray at home or have trouble reading their scripture. In this section you will learn which method of battle to utilize when facing certain obstacles in your life. Because this book is a revelation from Jesus Christ after reading it much deliverance will take place in your life. Be ready to be set free from any situation or problems you may be going through because only Jesus can deliver you through the power of his revelation.

1

Strategic Battle

*Then I arose in the night, I and a few men with me; I
told no one what my God had put in my heart to do at
Jerusalem; nor was there any animal with me, except
the one on which I rode*

Nehemiah 2:12 (NKJV)

Astrategic battle is a battle with a plan or method
of action that is designed to reach or acquire a goal
or solution. Throughout the bible we find many
characters that applied a strategic battle through instructions
given to them from God. In the book of Nehemiah 2:11-13
the bible said the wall of the city of Jerusalem was destroyed.
Nehemiah the servant of God moved by the Spirit of God
felt his calling as a warrior of God to rebuild the wall that
was destroyed. There were two spirits that fought against
Nehemiah, the spirits were Tobia and Samballa; they did not
want Nehemiah to rebuild the wall of Jerusalem. According
to the bible, Nehemiah went out at night in obedience to what
the Lord placed in his heart to do. He went and studied the
wall of Jerusalem; no one was with him or knew what he was
doing.

Nehemiah used a strategic battle to rebuild the wall. He
used this style to keep Tobia and Samballa from knowing
his plans. The bible lets us know, through the spirit of God
Nehemiah studied the wall at night, planning the resources he

would need for construction. Nehemiah was preparing himself for whatever would come his way while the construction was going on. Nehemiah studied where he needed strongmen, helpers, watchmen and other needed men. He studied the wall very close, learning the weak points and where more efforts were needed. Nehemiah knew every detail and was prepared for any attacks that would come his way.

In life there are some attacks that will come your way and a strategic battle is what is needed to fight the devil and win. God will give you instructions on how to fight the battle. There are times where God may lead you to pray at a park or a place other than your home. There are also times where God will instruct you to go on a fast for a certain period of time regarding that situation.

I recall a time God gave me specific instruction to give to my church, because the people were in need of cleansing. The instruction that was given was everyone in the ministry had to sleep with white clothing with a cross on it for five days. The white garment represented the people being cleansed and purified, making them white as snow. The cross represented the atonement of their sins, God's grace upon them and the blood of Jesus that was shed at the Calvary. During those five days people would tell me how demons tried to enter their homes. Some of the people experienced nightmares where they would see demons trying to touch them; others felt a demonic presence in their room. Because of their obedience nothing happened to any of them. At the end of those five days, many people received deliverance. Imagine if they chose to be disobedient and did not follow the instruction from God, they would have forfeited their blessings.

Strategic battle is needed to fight your enemy; you cannot keep fighting them the same way. In a football game if the team on offense continues to run the exact same plays over and over, then the other team would not have to figure out how to block their touchdown. In sports such as football the plays have to change up or else you forfeit your chance of winning.

Imagine if our military used the exact same tactics when at war, we would lose most of our battles. The same concept is needed when dealing with the enemy your prayer approach or technique must change. That is why it is important to be obedient in following the instructions God gives you.

A key to being successful at a strategic battle is through a sound mind. 2 Timothy 1:7 says "For God has not given us a spirit of fear, but of power and of love and of a sound mind." We have to use the sound mind that God gives us, a mind of super intelligence so we can fight the enemy with.

Prayer

Father, teach me how to strategically fight my enemies. Guide me with divine instruction on how to attack my enemies and bring victory in the mighty name of Jesus. Father I thank you for this revelation. Every fight that needs strategic battle in my life, lose your hold now in the name of Jesus, amen.

2

PROCESS BATTLE

You shall march around the city, all you men of war;
you shall go all around the city once. This you
shall do six days.

Joshua 6:3 (NKJV)

We have learned that a strategic battle involves in depth studying and planning towards achieving a goal, in this chapter we will be focusing on a process battle. A process is where different steps or methods are taken to achieve a certain end result. The process battle takes time it is a refinement or deliverance done over time. It can take days, weeks, months or even years before you receive a result. Jesus said some spirits can only be removed through fasting and praying (Matthew 17:21). There are times where God may lead you to pray at a certain time, for example praying every day at 5pm and on the 7th day you will have your victory; or a 21 day regimen where you receive your victory on the 21st day. Regardless of the regimen you are given, patience is needed.

In Joshua 6:2-5 God spoke to Joshua and told him to have the Israelites walk around Jericho once a day for seven days and on the seventh day at the sound of the trumpet the people are to make a loud shout and the wall of Jericho will collapse. God placed him in a Process Battle. A strategic battle focuses more on studying your enemy or playing smart by using the intelligence that God has given you through his Holy Spirit. A Process battle is just a process, you know after the process is over your miracle is guaranteed. Joshua did as the Lord commanded. It took Joshua seven days to win the fight and on the seventh day the bible tells us the wall of Jericho collapsed and they conquered Jericho.

There are times in your life where you will be faced with a process battle, whether the Lord leads you in one or you have to use one because of the tribulation or situation you are in, if not you will fail. You may question how effective this technique is and I have to say it really works, speaking from personal experience. I recall prior to God calling me into ministry there was a spirit I was fighting against and the Lord said instructed me to focus on prayer and attacking that spirit nonstop for three days. During that time period I was not to war against anything else but that spirit. Being obedient I began to do as the Lord commanded me. On the 3rd day I fought the spirit, I was dreaming and in my dream I saw the spirit inside of a church, I walked up to it and grabbed both of its hands, as I held its hands I said "in the name of Jesus every knee shall bow, at the name of Jesus every tongue must confess that Jesus Christ is Lord in heaven, over the earth and underneath the earth". After I said that the spirit immediately fell down and I woke up. Because of my victory over that demon I was able to enter into my ministry. God instructed me to use a process battle in order to win that fight.

You must be smart when you face something in your life to know what battle to apply in order to receive your victory in all your battle. When you are able to identify what battle to use I guarantee to you will not lose. Remember the battle belongs to the Lord.

3

CHALLENGING BATTLE

Now therefore, send and gather all Israel to me on
Mount Carmel, the four hundred and fifty prophets of
Baal, and the four hundred prophets of Asherah, who
eat at Jezebel's table

1 Kings 18:19 (NKJV)

In 1 Kings 18:22-24 we find the Prophet Elijah went on Mount Carmel and called up all the prophets of Baal and challenged them in the name of Jehovah. According to the bible Prophet Elijah went up and said to the prophets of Baal if their god is god to cause fire to come out from heaven and burn the sacrifice. Prophet Elijah said that if they were able to prove their god is god then all will follow their god, but if Prophet Elijah's God the true God causes fire to come out from heaven and burn the sacrifice then all will serve the Lord, the most High God. A challenge was set.

When the prophets of Baals called their god there was no answer, as you know the story when Elijah called his God the bible says fire came out from Heaven and burned the sacrifice. From that time on Prophet Elijah ordered that all the prophets of Baal be killed. This is what you call a challenging battle, a call to a fight. A challenging battle is where God shows his power. The bible said God hardened pharaoh's heart to demonstrate his mighty power as God, which is a challenging battle. A challenging battle is when God tells you to call your enemies and face them so that he can show his power and be glorified. When you are given an assignment like that you become fearless and stand with the power of God and contend with your enemy.

David said even though I walk through the valley of the shadow of death I shall fear no evil (Psalm 23). There are some situations in your life that God will tell you to challenge the devil and he will show up for you. So many times I go preach at places where the devil will come to bring disgrace and God will speak to me telling me to challenge them under his power and he shows up for me. When you can challenge your situation through the power of the Anointing of the Holy Spirit, they will not show up anymore. You need a warrior mind set, to challenge the devil with the anointing of Elijah by the spirit of The Lord. Challenging Battle is when you call your situation and say today we are going to see whose power is the greater power, the bible said the power that is in us is stronger than the power that is in the world.

A Challenging Battle is all about showing off the power of God, its all about showing off the God that you serve and what he is able or capable of doing. The enemy that is fighting you will flee in the name of Jesus. We cannot be afraid of demons, spirits, voodoo priest, witches, warlocks or free masons because the God we serve is Omnipotent and powerful. We need to be able to challenge our adversary in the name of Jesus for there is power in the name of Jesus. There are some spirits that will not leave unless you challenge them. There are some voodoo priests that will not stop fighting unless you challenge them under the power Of God. According to the bible we receive the Spirit without measure or unlimited power of God that is in us is in the fullness. We must challenge the devil and show the power of God.

Elijah challenged the false prophets and won. Do not be afraid of your enemy because your God is with you, the Battle belongs to the Lord.

Part Four

Prayers

Prayer for Forgiveness

Father in Heaven, you are holy. Forgive me for everything I have done wrong, my corrupt and negative words and things I was not supposed to say. Forgive me for my ignorance, and everything I have done wrong to anyone. Heavenly Father, forgive my disobedience towards you and men, in the Name of Jesus. I ask you to wash my sins and disobedience away with the blood of Jesus Christ. Holy Spirit, forgive me for everything I have done or said against you. Jesus, forgive me for everything I have done or said against you. Father, forgive me for everything I have done wrong to the angels. Father, touch me and prove to me that you hear me by signs and wonders. I renounce every contract I had with the enemy that has caused me to sin; I destroy them in Jesus name. Show me through signs and wonders every hidden covenant I had or have with the enemy. Every dark Angels following me your time ends here. I close every door I have sinfully opened and I open every door that I have sinfully closed, in the name of Jesus. Power of Sin, I destroy you and take authority over you. I bind every demonic spirit against me in the name of Jesus. Holy Spirit, empower me, my prayer life, my body, my thought, and my mind. I decree a new level in my life in Jesus name. I destroy every demonic dream, in Jesus name. Thank you Heavenly father, for hearing my prayer, I receive my total deliverance from sin and complete forgiveness in Jesus name. In Jesus Mighty name I pray, Amen!

O God Remember Me

O God Am I not Aggressive Enough?
Am I Being to Passive in Your Presence?
Is There a Curse that is upon me?
I cried for you Day and Night
I Look for you in the East but did not hear you
Has my Prayers Failed me?
Do you hear me When I Pray?
Have you given up on me?
O my God
You have promised me many things
I waited patiently
But none of them appeared to me
You have declared your word cannot be voided
Have you forgotten me?
O God, arise!
The enemy has blocked my way,
O God where are you?
Don't forget me
O God arise hear me, O Lord,
I am Calling unto you answer me
Don't ignore me
O God, hear my prayers,
Show me a sign that you are hearing me
My Father, My God please hear me,
Do not let me be alone in this dessert

O God, make your enemies my footstool
O God, do not take forever to answer me
But today answer me and rescue me
Remember me O God
I am ready to listen, I am ready to hear
I am ready to see what you want to do with me
I love you God my Father forever and ever
Amen

TAKE IT BACK

In the name of Jesus, everything the devil has taken from me
since Adam and Eve
I take it back through the blood of Jesus Christ
In the name of Jesus every spiritual gift from the Holy Spirit
the devil has stolen from me
I take it back through the blood of Jesus
In the name of Jesus every material blessing the devil
has taken from me
I take it back through the blood of Jesus
In the name of Jesus every satanic bank holding my money
I take my money back through the blood of Jesus
Through the blood of Jesus I claim my car in Jesus name
Through the blood of Jesus I claim my house in Jesus name
Through the Blood of Jesus I claim my possessions
in Jesus name
Through the Blood of Jesus I claim my deliverance
in Jesus name
Through the Blood of Jesus I claim my blessings in Jesus name
In the name of Jesus the wicked will not drive my car
In the name of Jesus the wicked will not sleep in my House
In the name of Jesus the wicked cannot touch my Marriage
In the name of Jesus the wicked will not touch my calling
In the name of Jesus the Wicked will not touch my destiny
In the Name of Jesus every wicked force in my car die
through the blood of Jesus

The thief against my life, die in the name of Jesus
Spiritual robbers against my life die in the name of Jesus
Liars against my life, die in the name of Jesus
Deceivers against my life, die in the name of Jesus
I renounce every contract with Spiritual Robbers in Jesus name
I renounce every contract with the thief in Jesus name

Prayer to Sleep at Night

Blood of Jesus cover me
Blood of Jesus cover my spirit
Blood of Jesus cover my soul
Blood of Jesus cover my body
Blood of Jesus cover my thought and mind
Blood of Jesus cover my house, dreams, my family, my bed,
my neighbor
In the mighty name of Jesus
According to Luke 10:19 I have receive authority to destroy
snakes and scorpions
And no power of the enemy will harm me in the mighty
name of Jesus.
According to Philippians 2:10, at the name of Jesus every
knee shall bow in heaven
On earth and under the earth.
Right now I stand according to Luke 10:19 and according to
Philippians 2:10 to pray this prayer in the name of Jesus
I command every dream manipulator be destroyed in the
mighty name of Jesus
I command every dream poison to be destroyed in the
mighty name of Jesus
I command every demonic dream to be destroyed in the
name of Jesus
I command every demonic riot in my dreams to be put to
confusion and destruction
In the mighty name of Jesus
I command every satanic secret agent,

Secret service or secret organization against my life to fall
down and die
In the mighty name of Jesus
I command every demonic ambush in my dreams to be put
to confusion and
Destruction in the mighty name of Jesus,
I command every traps, pits, and holes in my dreams be
destroyed in the mighty name of Jesus,
And I reverse them now
Let the enemy fall in them in Jesus name.
I command every demonic arrester be destroyed in the
mighty name of Jesus,
And I reverse them now in name of Jesus
Let the enemy fall in them in the name of Jesus
I Command every demonic arresters be destroyed in the
mighty name of Jesus
I arrest all my arresters in the mighty name of Jesus
Every chains of the enemy intended to bind me in my dreams I
break them in the name of Jesus Christ of Nazareth
Every Prison set up for me in my dreams
Be destroyed into irreparable pieces in the name of Jesus
I Command Every Satanic Cage set up for me be destroyed
into irreparable pieces in the mighty name of Jesus
Every thing the devil intended to steal in my dreams I cover
them in the blood of Jesus
I Command my inner man to fight the enemy in my dreams
in the mighty name of Jesus
I command my inner man to be strong in the mighty name
of Jesus
I arrest every Gun man in my dreams and bind them with
chains that cannot be broken
In the mighty name of Jesus
I command every satanic meeting that is being held against
me, be put into confusion
In the mighty name of Jesus

45

Any satanic agent summoning my name in the realm of the
spirit while I am sleeping
Fall down and die in the mighty name of Jesus
Every satanic secret organization calling my name from the
sea, earth and the heavenly
Fall down and die in the mighty name of Jesus
I command every evil observer from the hours of 12:00am to
3:00am to receive
Blindness in the mighty name of Jesus
I Command every spirit of Incubus and succubus to fall down
And be consumed in the mighty name of Jesus
I command the water in my body to boil to liquid fire in the
mighty name of Jesus
I command every spirit of heaviness attacking me while I'm
sleeping to receive total destruction in
the mighty name of Jesus
I take authority over the powers in the waters in the mighty
name of Jesus
Every attack of the enemy against my life in the moon the
sun the stars I destroy it and fire back in the
mighty name of Jesus
Every satanic program against my life in the moon, the sun
and the stars I deprogram it and I program success blessing
and every good thing from God in the name of Jesus
I destroy every witchcraft attack against my life and
I fire back to their senders in the name of Jesus
I destroy every voodoo attack against my life and I fire back
to their senders in the name of Jesus
I destroy every zombie attack against my life and I fire back
to their senders in the name of Jesus
Every star hunter against my life I put you to confusions fall
down now in the name of Jesus
Every star hijacker against my life I put you into confusion
fall down now in the name of Jesus
By the blood of Jesus I will remember my dreams in
Jesus mighty name

By the grace and favor of God I command the day to go in
my favor in Jesus mighty name
I command peace, joy and love to flood my day in the
mighty name of Jesus

Prayer to Command
The Element

In the name of Jesus every power from the element attacking any area of my life I destroy it in the mighty name of Jesus

Every power from the sea attacking my life I destroy it in the mighty name of Jesus

Every power from the wind attacking my life I destroy it in the mighty name of Jesus

Every power from the earth attacking my life I destroy it in the mighty name of Jesus

Every power from the fire kingdom inside of the earth attacking my life I destroy it in the mighty name of Jesus

Any satanic agent using the waters against my life I fire it back in the name of Jesus

Any satanic agent using the earth against my life I fire it back in the name of Jesus

Any satanic agent using the wind against my life I fire it back in the name of Jesus

Any satanic agent using wicked spirits against my life I fire it back in the mighty name of Jesus

I destroy Marine witchcraft against my life in the mighty name of Jesus

Any satanic agent using the earth as a satanic altar against me I destroy it in the mighty name of Jesus

Any satanic agent who is calling the Wind against me I destroy it in the name of Jesus

Any dark angels assigned against me fall down and die in the name of Jesus

Satanic agent of the earth against my life, fall down and die in the mighty name of Jesus

Satanic agent of the sea against my life, fall down and die in the mighty name of Jesus

Satanic agent of the power of the air against my life, fall down and die in the name of Jesus

Satanic prophet of the sea, fall down and die in the mighty name of Jesus

Satanic prophet of the earth, fall down and die in the mighty name of Jesus

Satanic prophet using wicked spirits against me fall down and die in the mighty name of Jesus

I break every water cauldron against my life by fire in the mighty name of Jesus

I break every fire cauldron against my life by fire in the mighty name of Jesus

I break every earth cauldron against my life by fire in the mighty name of Jesus

I break every air cauldron against my life by fire in the mighty name of Jesus

I render the tree powerless against my life by fire in the mighty name of Jesus

Let the east cooperate with me by fire in the mighty name of Jesus

Let the west cooperate with me by fire in the mighty name of Jesus

Let the north cooperate with me by fire in the mighty name of Jesus

Let the south cooperate with me by fire in the mighty name of Jesus

Foundational Prayer

Every foundational curse against me, I speak your destruction
in the name of Jesus

I build my foundation upon the Rock of Ages, in Jesus Name

Every foundational covenant against my Life, I speak your
destruction in the name of Jesus

My covenant is with God the Father, the Son and the Holy Spirit

Every foundational bondage against my life, I speak my
Liberty and freedom in the name of Jesus, loose your hold
upon my life in the name of Jesus

Every foundational arrester against my Life, I destroy you in
the name of Jesus, and I arrest you

For I receive power to bind and to loose in Jesus name

Every foundational darkness planted in my life I uproot you
now in the name of Jesus

Be consumed by the fire of the Holy Ghost

Every foundational serpent in my life, be consume by the fire
of the Holy Ghost in the name of Jesus

Every foundational scorpion in my life, be consume by the
fire of the Holy Ghost in the name of Jesus

Axe of God work in my foundation in the Mighty name of
Jesus

Every foundational witchcraft Attack against me I destroy it
in the name of Jesus and consume it by fire.

Blood of Jesus purge my foundation in the mighty name of
Jesus

Every foundational stronghold in my life, I speak your
destruction in the Mighty name of Jesus, For the Lord is
my strong tower and my fortress

Every foundational familiar spirit in my life, I destroy you in the mighty name of Jesus, and I receive the spirit of God in my life

Every foundational confusion, in my life I destroy you in the Mighty name of Jesus, and I receive the mind of Christ

Every foundational marine power against me, I destroy it in the mighty name of Jesus

Every problem attached to my family name I destroy it in the name of Jesus and I cover my name with the blood of Jesus.

ABOUT THE AUTHOR

Biography

Prophet Kervin Dieudonne is the general overseer of Prophetic Training Center and the pastor of The Worldwide Kingdom Ministry Inc., (Hebrews 12: 28-29). This church is located in Ft. Lauderdale Florida. Prophet Kervin was born in New York on October 14, 1988. He was raised in Haiti for his primary years. He returned to the states at the age of thirteen to complete his High School at Olympic Heights High School in West Palm Beach, Fl.

Prophet Kervin Dieudonne realized the call of God on his life at the age of 5 when he would get angelic visitations when he was in Haiti. The Lord began to visit him in dreams and visions about starting his own ministry in Fort Lauderdale. He served a man of God for 3 years. The commission the Lord gave him is a message to bring revival and light a fire in the world.

Gifted with a strong apostolic and office of prophetic, he flows in the anointing of teaching, healing, deliverance and prophecy. The Lord Jesus also gave him a personal vision that Prophet Kervin should prophesy restoration and life.

Jesus Christ has called him to preach the gospel to the nations. He has travelled to New York, Trinidad, Haiti, and Florida preaching the good news to the lost, proclaiming freedom for the captives and releasing from darkness the prisoners. A prophet is not known by his gift or his anointing, but by his fruit.